#POEMS

JUDGE THE POET

For Raney,
Enjoy!
Judge
XMAS '15

Copyright © 2015 Judge The Poet

All rights reserved.

ISBN: 1519226837
ISBN-13: 978-1519226839

FOR

CME, SOR AND ADR.

Contents

1. #One Love p.5
2. #Don't Jump p.7
3. #Awakening p.9
4. #Numbers p.11
5. #The Bank Of Life p.13
6. #Rat Race p.15
7. #Discover p.17
8. #Intellectual p.19
9. #Don't Apologise p.21
10. #What Are Poems? p.23
11. #Wars Are Over p.25
12. #Loss p.27
13. #Dream p.29
14. #Long View p.31
The Week
15. #Monday p.33
16. #Tuesday p.33
17. #Wednesday p.35
18. #Thursday p.35
19. #Friday p.35
20. #Blink p.37
21. #Hype p.39
22. #Alone p.41
23. #Don't p.43
24. #Listen p.45
25. #Modern Times p.47
26. #Imagination p.49
27. #Calm p.51
28. #Puzzle p.53
29. #Eyes Open p.55
30. #Think p.57
31. #Sense p.59

32. #Love's End p.61
33. #Do Something p.63
34. #Earth Is Flat p.65
35. #Foe p.67
Six Word Stories:
36. #6 Word Story 1   ......p.69
37. #6 Word Story 2   ......p.69
38. #6 Word Story 3   ......p.69
39. #6 Word Story 4   ......p.71
40. #6 Word Story 5   ......p.71
41. #6 Word Story 6   ......p.71
42. #Love p.73
43. #CrossWords p.75
44. #Scars p.77
45. #Politics p.79
46. #Good Morning p.81
47. #Doors p.83
48. #You p.85
49. #Sound And Vision p.87
50. #WW1   ......p.89
51. #Holiday p.91
52. #If p.93
53. #Society p.95
54. #For C.D. p.97
55. #Think First p.99
56. #Decision p.101
57. #How Poetry Works p.103
58. #Compassion p.105
59. #Perspective p.107
60. #The Balloon p.109
61. #Genes p.111
62. #Christmas 1914   ......p.113
63. #Poet p.115
64. #Right p.117

65. #As We Grow p.119
66. #Loneliness p.121
67. #Strictly Life p.123
68. #Shadows p.125
69. #The Camera p.127
70. #Once p.129
71. #Hope p.131
72. #21st Century p.133
73. #Growing p.135
74. #Correction p.137
75. #Wake Up p.139
Haikus:
76. Haiku 1: #Autumn p.141
77. Haiku 2: #Puddle p.141
78. Haiku 3: #Snowflake p.143
79. Haiku 4: #Consume p.143
80. Haiku 5: #Clouds p.143
81. #Golden Rule p.145
82. #Live p.147
83. #News p.149
84. #Forever p.151
85. #Smile p.153
86. #Trying p.155
87. #Words p.157
88. #Silent Noise p.159
89. #Cookies p.161
90. #Ladies And Gentlemen p.163
91. #Look p.165
92. #Christmas Eve p.167
93. #Empty p.169
94. #Recipe p.171
95. #Life p.173

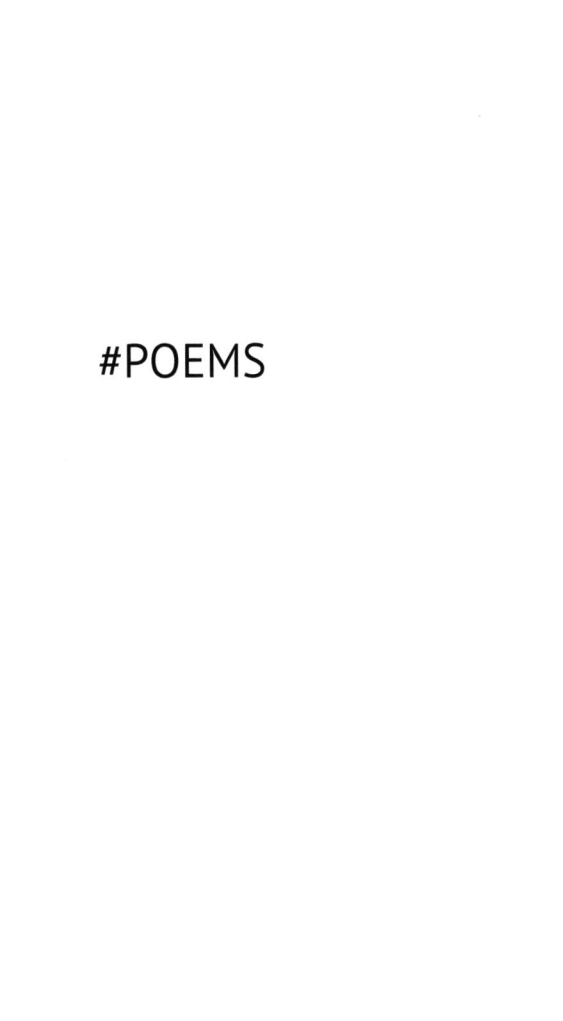

#POEMS

A COLLECTION OF SHORT POEMS

JUDGE THE POET

#POEMS

#One Love
Many cultures, rainbows of skin.
Let the end of hate begin.
With no difference life is duller,
And love loves every colour.

#Don't Jump

Don't jump in mango chutney
Or swim in piccalilli.
Getting into a pickle
Is really rather silly.

JUDGE THE POET

#Awakening
Catching first summer beams,
A small red rose bud dreams.
It opens and feels whole...
Sunshine fills the soul.

JUDGE THE POET

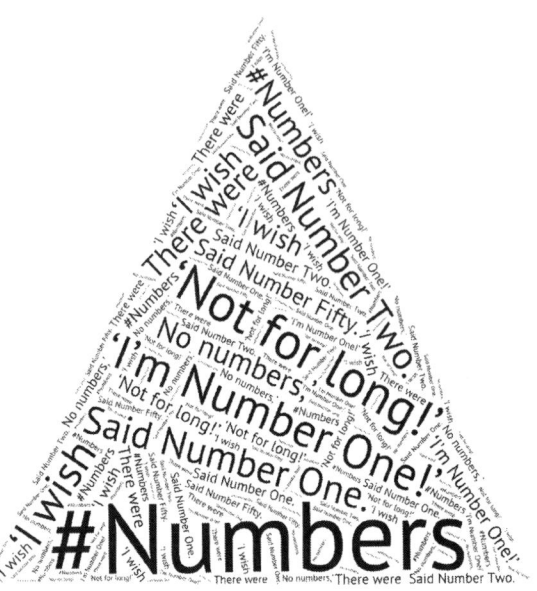

#Numbers

'I'm Number One!'
Said Number One.
'Not for long!'
Said Number Two.
'I wish
There were
No numbers,'
Said Number Fifty.

JUDGE THE POET

#The Bank Of Life
Health is wealth,
Love is riches,
Hope is a bridging loan.
Dreams hold your interest.

JUDGE THE POET

#POEMS

#Rat Race
Commute
Compute
Dispute
Dilute
Retire
Expire

#Discover
Shouting without anger,
Laughing without joy,
You will annoy.

Kindness without reward,
Love without condition,
Life's true mission.

JUDGE THE POET

#Intellectual
He did not drink wine.

Instead, the label read,
The bottle analysed,
He hypothesized.

Explaining,
Not understanding.

#Don't Apologise

Don't apologise
For being different.
Don't pretend
To be the same.

Variety
Is life's beauty.
Normality
Is just a game.

JUDGE THE POET

#What Are Poems?
As old as distant ages,
As fresh as love or deceit,
Spoken or written on pages,
The world within a heartbeat.

JUDGE THE POET

#Wars Are Over
Wars are over. Fighting done.
World comes together as one.
Politicians sent back to school.
Compassion reigns. April Fool.

#Loss
It's hard
To count your blessings
When there
Are tears in your eyes.

#Dream
If you dare to dream,
What will you find?
Imagination,
Wings for the mind.

JUDGE THE POET

#Long View

A patchwork quilt of fields
Nestles over jurassic hills.
May nature live to defeat
Our shallow, selfish wills.

JUDGE THE POET

(word-cloud shaped as a crescent moon and circle, containing phrases:)

The Week · **Monday** · **#Tuesday**

- Lives are not yet on repeat.
- Today is week's second child
- New week, a fresh blank sheet
- Yet we rage against Monday.
- Before dark midweek blues...
- Game on, let everyone play
- Shine on every goal you choose
- Pursue your dreams, go wild

The Week

#Monday
New week, a fresh blank sheet,
Lives are not yet on repeat.
Game on, let everyone play.
Yet we rage against Monday.

#Tuesday
Today is week's second child.
Pursue your dreams, go wild.
Shine on every goal you choose
Before dark midweek blues...

JUDGE THE POET

34

#Wednesday
Enjoy each day's new surprises,
Reject midweek midlife crisis.
No motorbike or trophy spouse.
Be a lion, not a cartoon mouse!

#Thursday
Two more days. Weekend beckons.
Count the hours, minutes, seconds.
As life's true professors say:
This is called Thirsty Thursday.

#Friday
Worries, the data life unlocks.
File them now. Delete that box.
Friday is life's clean sweeper:
Blessed beloved ungrim reaper.

JUDGE THE POET

Star-shaped word cloud composed of the repeated phrases:

#Blink · Nightly · So brightly · As bright · As the light · Recall when stars were seen · Please look up · They're still there. · Of an electric screen?

#Blink
Recall when stars were seen
So brightly
Nightly

As bright
As the light
Of an electric screen?

Please look up.
They're still there.

JUDGE THE POET

#Hype
Not all Italian coffee is good,
Not all French windows are French.
A discerning nose really should
Tell an aroma from a stench.

JUDGE THE POET

Wrecked by life,
The smile will not come.
He tries to smile.
And yet what
Do you call him:
Worthless, loser, bum?
#Alone

#Alone
Wrecked by life,
He tries to smile.
The smile will not come.

And yet what
Do you call him:
Worthless, loser, bum?

JUDGE THE POET

#Don't
Don't rock the boat or make a fuss.
Are you sure you're One Of Us?
All radical thoughts are barred.
Think. Believe. But not too hard.

JUDGE THE POET

A child's laugh
And is worth everything.
Is exactly how
World peace would sound.
A child's smile
Costs nothing
#Listen

#Listen
A child's smile
Costs nothing
And is worth everything.

A child's laugh
Is exactly how
World peace would sound.

JUDGE THE POET

#Modern Times
If Page 1 always updates,
You may never read Page 2.
What depth or understanding
Will then be hidden from you?

JUDGE THE POET

#Imagination
The heart-flutter of youth,
An icy-cold bath of truth,
Skies full of dancing birds,
Pictures painted with words.

JUDGE THE POET

#Calm

Such calm, rational voices.
Such calm, rational choices.
Invade. Kill. Smartbomb. Drone.
Greatest madness ever known?

JUDGE THE POET

Cleanliness is closer to #Puzzle Strangely, In most dictionaries, Debauchery than Godliness. Discuss.

#Puzzle
Strangely,
In most dictionaries,
Cleanliness is closer to
Debauchery than
Godliness.
Discuss.

JUDGE THE POET

#Eyes Open
All around us they pass by.
Everyday miracles never falter
Sunrise, sunset, baby's cry.

#Eyes Open
Everyday miracles never falter;
Sunrise, sunset, baby's cry.
Everyday miracles need no altar;
All around us they pass by.

JUDGE THE POET

A heart-shaped word cloud composed of the repeated phrases: "#Think", "Live young,", "Think old,", "Live old,", "Think young,", "You'll be old,", "You'll be love,", "Live love,", "Think love,"

#Think

Think old,
Live old,
You'll be old.

Think young,
Live young,
You'll be young.

Think love,
Live love,
You'll be love.

JUDGE THE POET

Warm, firm, Cool, hard. Ungiving, frigid. Delicious, yielding. Satisfies me the most. Is disappointing toast. #Sense

#Sense
Warm, firm,
Delicious, yielding,
Satisfies me the most.

Cool, hard,
Ungiving, frigid,
Is disappointing toast.

JUDGE THE POET

#Love's End

The end of a song.
The end of singing.
Sadness, when a love goes wrong.
Know, friend, it is not bringing

#Love's End

Sadness, when a love goes wrong.
The end of a song.
Know, friend, it is not bringing
The end of singing.

JUDGE THE POET

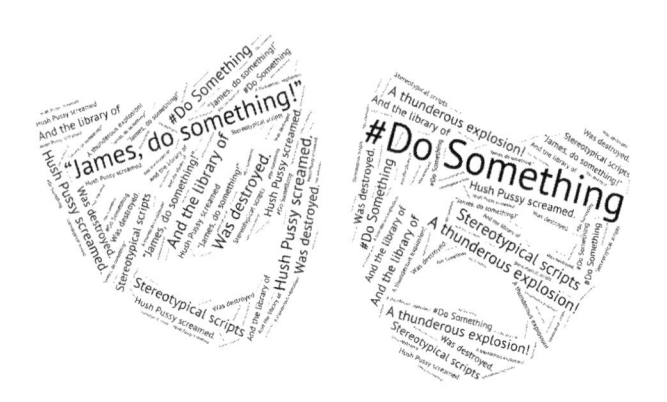

#Do Something
"James, do something!"
Hush Pussy screamed.
A thunderous explosion!
And the library of
Stereotypical scripts
Was destroyed.

JUDGE THE POET

#Earth Is Flat
Earth is flat. The moon is cheese.
Shakespeare could not rhyme it.
My three-eared cat has five knees.
Humans can't change climate.

JUDGE THE POET

#Foe
If the death of my foe or his child
Received the grief, deep and wild
Of a small star's death. The sorrow
Would end all war tomorrow.

JUDGE THE POET

Six Word Stories

#Six Word Story 1
Door closed.
Heart shattered.
Unsaid words.

#Six Word Story 2
Unnoticed caterpillar.
Love's cocoon.
Beautiful butterfly.

#Six Word Story 3
Sunday cloudy.
Family laughing.
Eternal sunshine.

JUDGE THE POET

#Six Word Story 4
Love letters.
Returned, unopened.
The end.

#Six Word Story 5
Accidental seed.
Sun. Rain.
Miraculous tree.

#Six Word Story 6
Baby cries.
Lover screams.
Death croaks.

JUDGE THE POET

There is magic in the air
And if you do not care
it will fly elsewhere.
Open hearts be aware.
#Love

#Love
Open hearts be aware:
There is magic in the air
And if you do not care
It will fly elsewhere.

JUDGE THE POET

Screaming for answers,
Every definition.
A craze filled mission.
Getting down, not across
#CrossWords

#POEMS

#CrossWords
Screaming for answers,
A craze filled mission.
Getting down, not across
Every definition.

JUDGE THE POET

#Scars

Life scars.
Blemished and marred
By sadness.
The beauty of youth
Is madness.
But to forget
Or even ignore
That true beauty
#Scars

#Scars
Life scars.
The beauty of youth
Blemished and marred
By sadness.

But to forget
Or even ignore
That true beauty
Is madness.

JUDGE THE POET

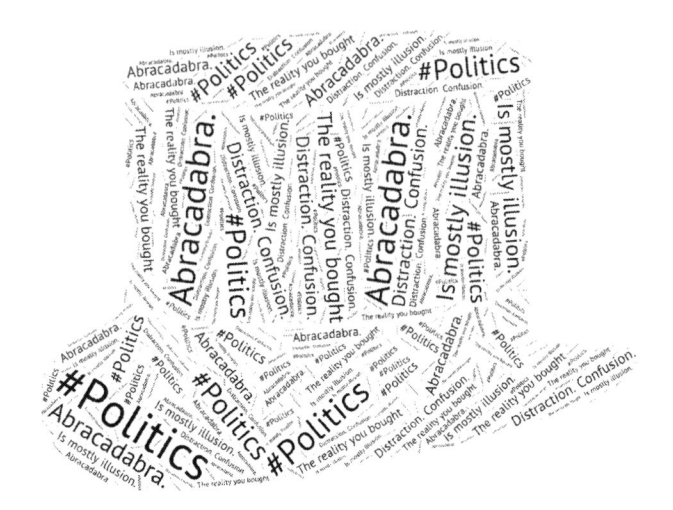

#Politics Abracadabra. Is mostly illusion. The reality you bought Distraction. Confusion.

#Politics
Abracadabra.
Distraction. Confusion.
The reality you bought
Is mostly illusion.

JUDGE THE POET

#Good Morning
Numberless stars
Close their eyes
As sunlit waves
Wash the horizon.
Cool air
Fills
With feathery song.

JUDGE THE POET

#Doors
The downcast pessimist trudged
Staring sombrely at the ground
And missed the opening doors
The up-looking optimist found.

JUDGE THE POET

There's a hole
#You
In my soul
Only
It can
Gets through
By you.
Be filled
Where the sin

#You

There's a hole
In my soul
Where the sin
Gets through.

It can
Only
Be filled
By you.

JUDGE THE POET

#Sound And Vision
With bright beauty and illusion,
TV is colourful confusion.
Radio's voice is a different kind,
Finding its truth inside the mind.

JUDGE THE POET

Word cloud in the shape of a hand containing the words:

#WW1 A flag Falling. Leaves from trees. Young men Ripped like Appalling. Conditions Waves in the breeze.

#WW1
Conditions
Appalling.
Young men
Falling.
Ripped like
Leaves from trees.
A flag
Waves in the breeze.

JUDGE THE POET

A word-cloud in the shape of a raindrop containing the phrases: #Holiday, Or rhyme, Whatever the season, Falls mainly, Without reason, The rain in England, All the time.

#Holiday
Whatever the season,
Without reason
Or rhyme,

The rain in England
Falls mainly
All the time.

JUDGE THE POET

#If winter is death,
Defying autumn's truth.
Then summer is love
And spring is youth,

#If
If winter is death
And spring is youth,
Then summer is love
Defying autumn's truth.

JUDGE THE POET

#Society
Privilege is an umbrella,
Protects in every weather.
So don't believe the fella
Says we're all in this together.

JUDGE THE POET

The Day But One Before Yesterday's Newspaper.
Charles Dickens,
And insight.
With delight.
#For C.D.
Glaring details, care
Expectations shared

#For C.D.
Charles Dickens,
The Day But One Before
Yesterday's Newspaper.

Glaring details, care
And insight.
Expectations shared
With delight.

JUDGE THE POET

A careless word or act
Can land you
In deep water.
Once you've kissed
The vicar's daughter
You can't go back to church

#Think First

#Think First
A careless word or act
Can land you
In deep water.

You can't go back to church
Once you've kissed
The vicar's daughter.

JUDGE THE POET

#Decision
Reach out and do what you can
Or pursue ego, self to please?
United caring could be our plan.
Selfishness is our worst disease.

JUDGE THE POET

#How Poetry Works
Words
Saying
Arrange these
Into
A well known
Or
Expression.

JUDGE THE POET

#Compassion

Someone calls out,
Voice full of pain.
We just pass by.
They call out again.

A tree blossoms
With colour and life.
We cut it down,
A blood-stained knife.

Compassion's a gift,
Lives in us all.
The test by which
We stand or fall.

Simplest feelings
Can be strongest.
Sweetest dreams
Can last longest.

Make your own choice,
Which is the way?
Live with compassion,
Starting today?

JUDGE THE POET

A shaped poem in the form of a wine glass, composed of the repeated lines:

From glass old or new.
A small stain
#Perspective
A good wine
Will still taste fine.
We are who we are.
On the window pain
Does not spoil a view.

#Perspective
A small stain
On the window pain
Does not spoil a view.

A good wine
Will still taste fine
From glass old or new.

We are who we are.

JUDGE THE POET

#The Balloon
There is a beauty in its
Shrinking, wrinkling demise,
Recalling youthful firmness
Thrust high in party skies.

JUDGE THE POET

#Genes
Shaken
The kaleidoscope of life.
Colours and shapes
Into unique personalities,
By chance and design.
Haven't we met before?

#Genes
The kaleidoscope of life.

Colours and shapes
Shaken
Into unique personalities,
By chance and design.

Haven't we met before?

JUDGE THE POET

Out of the trench,
#Christmas 1914
Sad human eyes.
Weapons fall still.
Bullet grey skies.
Hope one, War nil.
War's sickly stench.

#Christmas 1914
War's sickly stench,
Bullet grey skies.
Out of the trench,
Sad human eyes.

Weapons fall still.
Hope one, War nil.

JUDGE THE POET

#Poet
I've never been a handyman
To put up shelves and rails.
I simply try and fix things
With rhyme glue and word nails.

JUDGE THE POET

#Right

I'm bigger than you,
I must be right.
I'm bigger than you,
Want to fight?

See my fist,
Feel its might.
Grim darkness,
Endless night.

JUDGE THE POET

#As We Grow

If, as we grow and age,
A square,
Seems more like
The circle of life.
We look down,
We look across,
We look back,
We look up,
Then the circle of life.

#As We Grow
If, as we grow and age,

We look up,
We look across,
We look down,
We look back.

Then the circle of life
Seems more like
A square.

JUDGE THE POET

Human interaction:
The soul.
#Loneliness
Nourishing,
Diminishing
Makes whole.

#Loneliness
Human interaction:
Nourishing,
Makes whole.

Loneliness is acid,
Diminishing
The soul.

JUDGE THE POET

#Strictly Life

Muscle memory, movement set,
Learn to learn and then forget:
Relax as rhythm fills your soul
And you'll reach a glittery goal.

JUDGE THE POET

As we walk in the light,
Things we should have done
But didn't,
Are shadows attached
To our souls
#Shadows

#Shadows
Things we should have done
But didn't,
Things we should not have
But did,

Are shadows attached
To our souls
As we walk in the light.

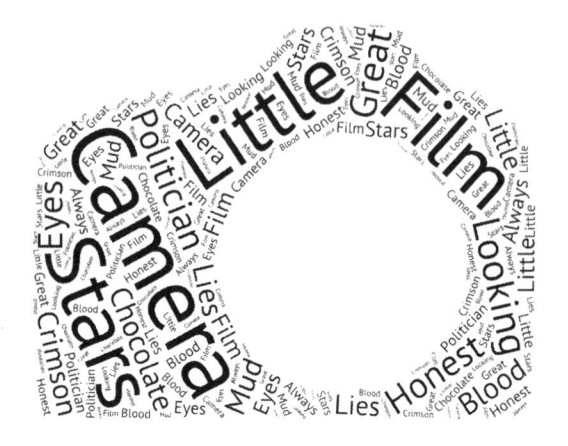

#The Camera
Little film stars looking great,
An honest politician's eyes,
Crimson blood on chocolate mud.
The camera always lies.

JUDGE THE POET

#Once

Once
We came
From the same place.

Then
We spread
And we changed.

Today
We again
Intermingle.

One people,
One love,
Onederful.

JUDGE THE POET

#Hope
I resist the fist
With which you knock, sir.
I am a peaceful one
And not a boxer.

#Hope
I resist the fist
With which you knock, sir.
I am a peaceful one
And not a boxer.

JUDGE THE POET

Misogeny.
Caution creatives;
#21st Century
Casual
Fine progeny
Doesn't display
Beware your

#21st Century

Caution creatives:
Beware your
Fine progeny

Doesn't display
Casual
Misogeny.

JUDGE THE POET

Word cloud in the shape of a running figure, composed of the phrases: Which hide, Beneath, Falling teeth, Deep inside, #Growing, I take care of, And the future., Honours me., The growing child, Runny noses, Wisdom.

#Growing

The growing child
Honours me.

I take care of
Falling teeth
Beneath
Runny noses

Which hide,
Deep inside,
Wisdom
And the future.

JUDGE THE POET

#Correction
To serve the many (not money),
As we look for hope (not hype).
Dear modern world autocorrect,
You are simply not our type...

JUDGE THE POET

Skies with bombers leaden.
Politicians talking.
Ignorance sleepwalking
Into armageddon.
#Wake Up

#Wake Up
Politicians talking.
Skies with bombers leaden.
Ignorance sleepwalking
Into armageddon.

JUDGE THE POET

Haikus

Haiku 1: #Autumn
Waving branches strain
Farewell, summer leaves.

Haiku 2: #Puddle
Under cold autumnal rain.
An empty puddle.
Or is it a hole?
Is that really a puddle?

Haikus

Haiku 1: #Autumn
Waving branches strain
Under cold autumnal rain.
Farewell, summer leaves.

Haiku 2: #Puddle
An empty puddle.
Is that really a puddle?
Or is it a hole?

JUDGE THE POET

Haiku 3: #Snowflake
Pen invisible.
Design unpredictable.
Perfection precise.

Haiku 4: #Consume
London, Saturday.
Christmas shoppers all about.
Greed, Greed, Greed, Greed, Greed.

Haiku 5: #Clouds
Ghostly floating forms,
Changing observers of Earth.
What if clouds could speak?

JUDGE THE POET

#Golden Rule
Let your glowing heart reign,
That is the Golden Rule.
Love is grace and comfort
For both wise man and fool.

JUDGE THE POET

#Live
Wonder
Question
Dream
Believe
Achieve
Inspire.

JUDGE THE POET

#News

It's nothing to do with me.
Food on table, sleep is free.
Not my problem, don't ask more.
Who's that knocking at my door?

JUDGE THE POET

Crops grow, giving grain.
Clouds clash, bringing rain.
Hearts crash, bringing pain.
Life falls, to rise again.
#Forever

#Forever
Clouds clash, bringing rain.
Crops grow, giving grain.
Hearts crash, bringing pain.
Life falls, to rise again.

JUDGE THE POET

#Smile

Smile.

Make false promises
To those
Whose
Votes you need.

Disappoint,
By acting
More
Like you believe.

Mutual dislike.

Repeat.

JUDGE THE POET

#Trying
Life often fails a hopeful test,
Looking for justice everywhere.
Just dream, believe and do your best
And be the one who tries to care.

JUDGE THE POET

Many words.
Words, words,
Already have seen.
#Words
See
Mirror
Or mirage?
Is to help us
What we should
The writer's role
What do they mean?

#Words

Words, words,
Many words.
Mirror
Or mirage?
What do they mean?

The writer's role
Is to help us
See
What we should
Already have seen.

JUDGE THE POET

Tapping and swiping.
They sit in a circle,
#Silent Noise
Glassy eyed,
Separated
By communication.

#Silent Noise
They sit in a circle,
Glassy eyed,
Tapping and swiping.

Separated
By communication.

Cookies
Dipping
Coffee
Risk
Sunk
Biscuit
Really
Gingerly
Takes
Overdunk

#Cookies
Dipping cookies in my coffee,
So gingerly I risk it.
Overdunk and you are sunk
Which really takes the biscuit.

JUDGE THE POET

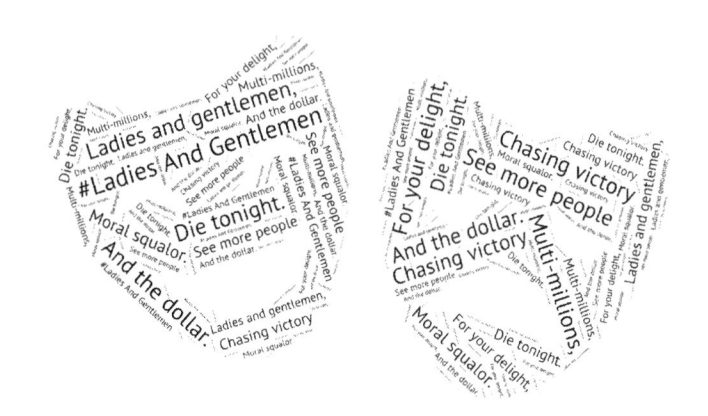

#Ladies And Gentlemen

Ladies and gentlemen,
For your delight,
See more people
Die tonight.

Chasing victory
And the dollar.
Multi-millions,
Moral squalor.

JUDGE THE POET

#Look
We hide from it
As if scared.

Worship is not
Acceptance.

Cosmetics are
Empty dreams.

Beauty is everywhere.

JUDGE THE POET

#Christmas Eve
Is like
A cloud.
Of shining ice.
Are the crystals
In clouds?
Do you believe
Santa Claus
Is like
Belief, goodness,
Giving and hope

#Christmas Eve
Santa Claus
Is like
A cloud.

Belief, goodness,
Giving and hope
Are the crystals
Of shining ice.

Do you believe
In clouds?

JUDGE THE POET

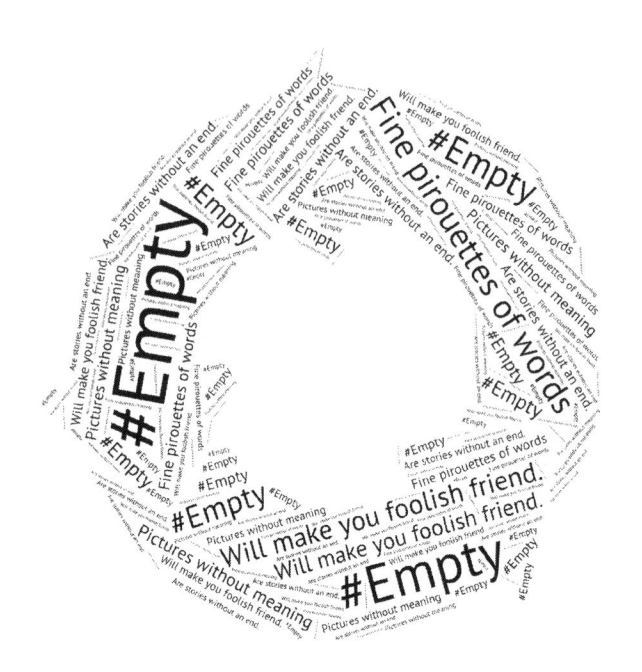

Fine pirouettes of words
Are stories without an end
Pictures without meaning
Will make you foolish friend.
#Empty

#Empty
Fine pirouettes of words
Will make you a foolish friend.
Pictures without meaning
Are stories without an end.

JUDGE THE POET

#Recipe
Take one vessel,
Pour in four spirits,
Cook slowly.

Nurture, educate,
Confuse, disappoint,
Amaze, love.

Place before mirror.

JUDGE THE POET

#Life
Life is for living,
Love is for-giving,
Dreams are for achieving,
And the future starts here.